Extreme SPORTS
Almanac

by Dan Koeppel

ROXBURY PARK

LOWELL HOUSE JUVENILE

LOS ANGELES

NTC/Contemporary Publishing Group

Photos provided by AllSport USA and Ride Publishing.

Cover photos © AllSport USA. All rights reserved.

Published by Lowell House

A division of NTC/Contemporary Publishing Group, Inc.
4255 West Touhy Avenue, Lincolnwood (Chicago),
Illinois 60646-1975, U.S.A.
© 1998 by Lowell House

Roxbury Park is a division of NTC/Contemporary Publishing
Group, Inc.

Lowell House books can be purchased at special discounts
when ordered in bulk for premiums and special sales.
Contact Customer Service at the following address:
NTC/Contemporary Publishing Group
4255 W. Touhy Avenue
Lincolnwood, IL 60646-1975
1-800-323-4900

ISBN: 0-7373-0032-9
Library of Congress Cataloging-in Publication Number: 98-066145

Managing Director and Publisher: Jack Artenstein
Editor in Chief, Roxbury Park Books: Michael Artenstein
Director of Publishing Services: Rena Copperman
Managing Editor: Lindsey Hay
Designer: S. Pomeroy

Printed and bound in the United States of America
10 9 8 7 6 5 4 3 2 1

To my mom and dad
Special thanks to Zapata Espinoza, who gave
me my start in extreme sports
--D.K.

Contents

What Is an Extreme Sport, Anyway?

1

Years ago most people thought of sports as something you did on a team: You played basketball, or baseball, or football. These sports were fun, but they usually required a lot of organization and planning. But there have also been sports that were individually oriented—things people did, usually by themselves, usually outdoors, and often with an eye toward experiencing nature.

The first true extreme sport was surfing. Riding a wooden board on the waves has been practiced in the South Pacific for many years, and it has appealed to people who think independently and see sports as a form of self-expression, as a way of getting in touch with their wilder sides.

That's what's so great about extreme sports: Though some of them can be dangerous, they're usually about being an individual. And while superstars like Michael Jordan bring creativity to team sports, in an extreme sport you don't have to be a superstar to be creative. You just have to be willing to try something new, to do things the way you think they should be done.

Surfing gave birth to two of the most popular extreme sports of today: skateboarding and snowboarding. Many extreme sports are also the product of advanced technology. BMX, mountain biking, and in-line skating all came into being when the time was right, when different ideas merged to make new inventions possible. In BMX it was kids imitating motorcycle racers. In mountain biking it was the availability of techniques originally used to build airplanes

and spacecraft. Bike inventors used them to make their products stronger and lighter than ever before. In in-line skating (and skateboarding, too) it was the development of new kinds of rubber and ball bearings that made for better, smoother-rolling wheels, adding speed and control to the more raw, earlier versions of the sports.

During the early part of this century, when team sports were growing, many people either lived in cities or on farms. People in cities didn't have a lot of places to play, so organized teams were important if people wanted to get any exercise at all. And farms had a lot of open space, so people could get together after work and make a football or baseball field. But after World War II, people started living in suburbs. Their lives became more structured. They looked for things to do after work or school. The wide sidewalks and carefully planned parks made transportation by bike and skateboard more convenient. Easy access to cars and freeways made weekend trips—to the desert to ride motorcycles, or to the ocean to surf—something everyone could do.

This all leads to a simple question: What is an extreme sport? There are lots of definitions, and many of them center around a sport that's wild or dangerous. But that may not be the best definition, because most extreme sports are not really that dangerous if you're careful and take the time to be safe. A better definition might be any individual sport that people pursue with a passion. Many mountain bikers, for example, identify themselves as mountain bikers, meaning that whether they're college students, doctors, or plumbers, they still think of themselves on their bikes first.

Extreme sports are connected to nature. This is true even if you're riding a skateboard in the middle of a city! When extreme enthusiasts talk about nature, they're really talking about movement—a feeling that they're in control of what they do and where they go. This can happen on concrete. It can happen on snow. It can happen on dirt.

Some extreme sports seem very silly. A lot of people point to bungee jumping as an example of something that's not really a sport at all. We tend to agree. Though the family of extreme sports might include wacky stunts, real extreme sports are ones that involve real exercise, real passion, and real movement. Though they are often outrageous, they're not about *being* outrageous.

It's a subtle difference. Try any extreme sport and you'll get the picture.

I hope that, as you learn about extreme sports, you'll also remember that many of these activities can help change the world. When more and more people surf or snowboard, for example, they learn about protecting the environments they're exploring. When machines once used to build airplanes are turned toward making bicycles, new jobs are being created—and the entire planet is made a better, safer place.

That's why many people think that extreme sports are the future of sports. They're something anybody with a little time and a little enthusiasm can do, and enjoy.

I hope you like reading this book about extreme sports as much as I enjoyed writing it.

Extreme Safety

2

Okay, now you know what an extreme sport is. Now let's talk about how to do them without getting hurt. First of all, remember that the pros do get injured sometimes. That's part of their job, and they're paid well to take those risks. They spend their entire lives building their skills to the point where those risks are manageable.

You don't have to. Even if you want to be a pro, you'll never get there if you get seriously injured. In fact, the best way to get better is to stay healthy. Here are some basic safety rules that apply to all extreme sports:

1 *Know your limits.* This is the most important rule in any extreme sport, whether you're climbing a mountain, surfing the ocean, or skateboarding downtown. Knowing what you are and aren't capable of actually makes you better at your sport. It gives you the ability to understand when you're ready to move on to the next level.

2 *Control the risk.* Mountain bike racers always pre-ride the courses they compete on. Dirt jumpers always watch others jumping before they make an attempt. The point is that knowing all the variables increases your chances of success—and decreases the chance of injury.

3 *Keep your equipment in perfect shape.* Top pros in all extreme sports have one advantage over amateurs: access to new, perfectly maintained equipment. Even though most people have to take care of their own gear (instead of having a mechanic or a factory representative deal with it for them), you can still give yourself the pro advantage by knowing how your gear works and what it takes to keep it in shape, and making sure that you never go out with anything that's not in complete working order.

4 *Wear safety gear.* Different extreme sports have different attitudes about safety gear. But that's changing. Whether it's biking or skateboarding, helmets are essential. Other sports require additional specialized safety equipment. You should know what's needed to keep you protected from accidents and the elements in any sport you choose. (You'll learn more about this in later chapters.)

5 *Let people know.* Planning a mountain bike ride in the hills? Going to the skate park? Use the buddy system. That means always doing your sports with somebody who can go for help if there's a problem, and who can (of course!) get better at the sport with you. The buddy system isn't just safer—it's more fun. It's also important always to always tell somebody at home where you're planning to go and when you'll be back.

6 *Understand the environment.* Many of the places where extreme sports are practiced can be dangerous. The ocean, for example, may look calm on the surface but may hold powerful tides and currents. Or wild animals may be in the forest, just beyond your view. Part of the joy of extreme sports is how they combine with nature. It's important to respect that nature, and prepare for it. If you take the time to learn about nature's power, you'll become more powerful yourself.

7 *Prepare for the unexpected.* The thing that compounds injury is not knowing what to do when bad luck hits. Many mountain bikers and snowboarders have gotten lost or hurt and saved themselves by being resourceful, by having prepared in advance, and, most importantly, by remaining calm. Always have a plan in case something unexpected happens. A plan can be as simple as just asking yourself: "What would I do if . . . ?"

8 *Respect others.* Many of the best extreme sports playgrounds are also crowded. There's nothing scarier than a high-speed mountain biker coming at a hiker or a horseback rider. In surfing there's nothing more annoying than being the first one in line for the next wave and having somebody cut in front of you. Remember, we share our sports and our favorite places with the rest of the world. Take care that you leave a good impression. Respect others on waves and trails, and always pay attention.

Getting Started

hat if you want to try getting into an extreme sport? There are so many to choose from, and they seem very intimidating at first. Here are some general hints:

1 *Find a friend.* If there's a particular sport you're interested in and you know somebody who's already good at it, it would be smart to get that person's advice. There's nothing better than having others help you figure things out, and they might also have some used equipment you can practice on!

2 *Ask questions.* There's no such thing as a stupid question. If you don't know something, just ask. One very good place to have your questions answered is your local sports shop. Your neighborhood bike mechanic or skate salesperson will be happy to help you understand anything that isn't clear.

3 *Read up.* Besides books like this, most extreme sports have whole magazines dedicated to them. Sometimes the magazines can be a little intimidating to beginners, because everybody in them seems so good. Don't worry.

There's plenty of valuable information you can pick up while you're looking at one of those glossy, color action magazines. They quickly help you become familiar with the people, places, and equipment associated with your sport.

4 *Don't burn out.* One of the biggest mistakes beginners make is going too hard. They get very excited by the sport, do it constantly for a few weeks—and then give it up. You don't have to spend every minute of your life on your skateboard. Build slowly and steadily, learning all the basics as you go.

5 *Make it part of your life.* There are great ways to make your favorite sport a real part of every day. Ride your bike to school instead of taking the bus. Get a scouting merit badge in your sport. Go to a summer camp that has lessons in the sport you've chosen.

6 *Involve your family.* Here's a secret: If you involve your parents, they will understand your new sport better and probably will be more willing to help you out. One bike racer tells us that when he started out, he wanted a new bike, so he asked his mom to go biking with him. She liked it so much that she bought the racer his new bike! (Besides, think how funny and weird your dad would look on a skateboard.)

7 *Get good.* One of the best things about extreme sports is that you get to define how good you want to be.

There's a wonderful moment in every activity when you suddenly realize: "Hey, I know how to do this." It takes practice and hard work, but it's worth it.

8 *Take a lesson.* If you find that you need more help, or have reached a plateau of skills that you just can't seem to get past, try taking a lesson. Snowboard and mountain bike lessons are often available at ski areas, and other sports have teachers, camps, and schools that advertise in magazines.

An Extreme Olympian:
An Interview with Susan DeMattei

Susan DeMattei is a perfect example of somebody who loved her extreme sport so much that she made a whole career of it. Starting when she was in her twenties, she began mountain biking while working as a registered nurse. She went all over the world, met her husband, and in 1996 won the bronze medal in the Olympics! Susan is retired from competitive biking now. She's still working as a nurse, but she also teaches mountain biking to kids and comments on mountain bike races for the Outdoor Life Network.

Q: How did you decide to become an extreme athlete?

A: When I was ten or eleven, I started getting into gymnastics, and I really loved that. That was the era of Olga Korbut and Nadia Comaneci [two Olympic superstars], and I was very enthralled with it. I kind of had aspirations of going to the Olympics some day in gymnastics. But when I got to high school, it became more obvious I wasn't going to be good enough at it.

Q: Then what happened?

A: Well, I'm embarrassed to say I was fairly inactive in high school, which I regret to this day—I didn't even think about doing any team sports. When I went to college, I got into exercise. I did a lot of running and cycling. But after that gymnastics disappointment, it never occurred to me that I could be in the Olympics.

Q: But then you started mountain biking?

A: Yes, but even then I didn't think I'd become a professional. This was in the 1980s, and nobody thought it could become an Olympic sport. I raced until 1994, and I had planned to retire, but then somebody told me it would be in the 1996 Olympics, so I decided to try for that.

Q: And you ended up winning a bronze medal!

Susan DeMattei

A: It was amazing. I still can't believe it happened!

Q: Do people think it's surprising that you quit after that and went back to being a nurse?

A: Maybe, but I'm glad. Being an athlete is great, but it's very selfish, in a way. You have to be all about yourself. I wanted to expand my horizons and do something for others.

Q: So you're glad you learned a career before you became a professional athlete?

A: I don't want to sound like a preacher, but I always feel compelled to say that you need something to fall back on. It's important to follow through with high school and college. You never know what might happen. You could get injured, or there might be another reason to get out, and you need something to do at that point.

Q: What kind of advice do you have for kids?

A: Well, most of them grew up with extreme sports, so a lot of them have even better skills than me. The most important thing is the need for safety. It's your responsibility to make sure your gear is working correctly and to know the rules of the road or trail. I always try to tell people to incorporate respectfulness and responsibility into their activity. You can't separate them from the action.

Q: And do it for fun, right?

A: It's really important to highlight the fun of any sport. I love sports for so many reasons—they're fun, healthy, something you can do with your friends and your family. They're also good for the environment. And I think you can really learn from them: It's like home-work—you make little goals for yourself. You ride a little farther each time, or practice something you couldn't do until you're good at it. That helps teach you for life.

Surfing

I t is the oldest extreme sport in the world, and it is the sport that, in modern times, defines what an extreme activity is: thrilling, individualistic, and full of creativity. Though many people think surfing is limited to Hawaii and California, the truth is that it has become a worldwide sport. Anywhere there's a beach (or a wave pool)—from Australia to Peru or France, or even New York City—you'll find surfers.

HOW SURFING CAME TO BE

Surfing started hundreds—maybe thousands—of years ago. Some people think the first surfers were from what is now Peru; others say Africa; still others say Polynesia. What is certain is that the first surfers we really know about were from the South Pacific. To them, riding the waves on boards called *alala* was not just fun—it was religious, and part of their worship of the sea.

Surfing first came to the awareness of people in the United States in the late 1800s, when they began to hear stories about a faraway Pacific island called Hawai'i. (Today we call it Hawaii.) By the early 1900s people all over the world had heard about the strange and mystical sport of riding waves. In 1907 George Freeth became one of the first people to introduce surfing to Southern California.

The craze began. One of the most famous surfers of the early days was Duke Kahanamoku, who also won a gold medal at the Olympics for swimming. Duke was the perfect Hawaiian surfer. One of his most important inventions was the modern longboard—a surfboard big enough for two people. For the first time, couples could surf together and beginners could learn on the same board as more experienced teachers. Duke also helped export surfing all around the world. When he visited Australia he started a surfing craze.

U.S. Open, Huntington Beach, California.

In the United States, the craze continued with the introduction of Tom Blake's hollow surfboard. This made the sport easier, and people in Southern California caught the fever. (Southern California plays heavily in the history of surfing. The good weather, accessible beaches, and large population made it the perfect place for the sport to explode.) People were discovering that surfing was something special—not just because it was fun, but because it brought people together, and brought them closer to the sea.

One of the most famous spots in surfing was (and still is) Malibu, just north of Los Angeles. It was there, during the 1960s, that the term "hotdog" came into being. Hotdogging is doing tricks on a surfboard, riding with style—a kind of showing off. Extreme sports are all about hotdogging!

The other important thing that happened to surfing in the 1960s was a documentary movie called *The Endless Summer*. In this film, Bruce Brown traveled the world looking for places to surf. It perfectly captured the free spirit of the sport and also gave birth to legions of surf photographers, writers, and filmmakers who realized that documenting their sport was a good way to make a living.

At the same time, a popular movie called *Gidget* opened the door to dozens of "beach party" movies that brought a Hollywood version of the surfing lifestyle—complete with music, dancing, fashion, and cars—to people who didn't live anywhere near the ocean. It made them want to surf, too. Such films popularized the notion of "surf culture." Surfing was the first real extreme sports culture. The people who did it loved it so much that it became the most important part of their lives.

Today's surf world is very professionalized. There are giant competitions, world tours, and many surf superstars who make big bucks. But it is also very friendly. Thousands of "regular" people surf daily, and still see it as an important commitment to the planet. Organizations like the Surfrider Foundation, an environmental group that works on ocean preservation, prove that surfers not only love their sport but are dedicated to cleaning up their environment as well.

All About Surfboards

The earliest surfboards were made from carved wood. Today's board *looks* somewhat the same, but in every other way it is different. Modern surfboards are usually made of fiberglass, foam, and wood, and the shape and length of the board are matters of individual preference, though today's boards are considerably shorter

Surfboards come in all shapes and sizes.

than the ones used by Duke Kahanamoku. Here are some famous surfboards from history:

Olo. These ancient boards were made from the Willwill tree, and were used only by kings and royalty. They were really long—up to twenty feet! The "common" board was called the *Alaia*, made from the koa tree.

Tom Blake's hollow boards. Until the 1930s, most surfboards were made of heavy, solid wood. They were very hard to paddle. When Tom Blake got the idea to make a hollow board, most people laughed—until they saw him surfing! He could surf all day long without getting tired because he was using less effort to get out to the waves.

Hot curl surfboards.

These boards were an evolution from Blake's hollow boards but with a narrow tail. This made the board much more maneuverable. Why was that important? Until the invention of the hot curl board, surfers usually rode straight ahead, in front of a wave. With hot curl boards, surfers learned how to move, making it possible for them to ride *inside* a wave. That's what modern surfing is all about: moving within, rather than in front of, the waves.

Fiberglass surfboards.

After World War II, lots of new technology became available to the public. One new material was fiberglass, a kind of plastic that

Some boards come with straps to attach your feet to the board.

World-famous Waimea Bay, Hawaii.

was easy to mold. Several surf designers saw that, by combining fiberglass with different kinds of wood, they could create lighter boards with sleeker, more efficient shapes.

The Hobie board. Before Hobie, most boards were made of balsa wood layered with fiberglass. The problem was that balsa was rare and expensive. Surfboard designer Hobie Alter was one of the first to realize that foam—blown into place and then shaped— would be a perfect surfboard material. The techniques Hobie developed are still in use—if you buy a surfboard today, it would still be remarkably like the ones Hobie made in the 1950s.

The shortboard. The modern surfboard is built like the Hobie, but it is much shorter. The shortboard completed the evolution of surfboards to where they are today: superlight, supermaneuverable, and capable of amazing things—if the right person is riding!

FAMOUS SURFING PLACES AND PEOPLE

Like most extreme sports, there are special locations in surfing that every surfer dreams about visiting—and the people who master these places become the sport's most famous personalities.

Three Amazing Places

Waimea Bay, Kauai, Hawaii. This is probably surfing's most legendary spot. Only the best can surf Waimea, because the waves there are huge and scary. Waimea represents the highest, hardest form of surfing: riding the biggest waves in the world.

Mavericks, Santa Cruz, California. This is one of the classic big-wave beaches in Northern California. The water's very cold at Mavericks, so most riders wear wet suits. It is definitely not for beginners. In fact, there are probably only twenty or thirty surfers in the world good enough to master the big swells at Mavericks.

The Pipeline, North Shore, Oahu, Hawaii. This is also one of surfing's most perfect spots, where the waves curl forward in a beautiful "pipe" that the best surfers actually ride into, moving through it the way a car moves through a tunnel.

Kelly Slater

Two Super Surfers

Kelly Slater. Florida legend Kelly Slater is currently perhaps the world's best surfer. Slater is known for his incredible competitive drive. He is the first surfer to make $1 million in a single season. He also co-starred on the TV series *Baywatch* for two seasons!

Lisa Anderson. Today's top woman surfer, Anderson is also from Florida. She's known for her bravery and daring. She was one of the

With so many people on a wave at once, it's important to observe surfing etiquette.

first women to ride the big waves at Mavericks and Waimea, and one of the first to insist that she be judged against all surfers, of either gender. She asks for no special treatment, and doesn't get any. What she does get is respect from every other surfing pro, because Lisa—a three-time world champion—is the real thing.

BASIC EQUIPMENT AND TRICKS

Tools and Techniques Beginners Should Know

Surfboard. Both longboards (over nine feet) and shortboards are popular these days. A good board for beginners is called a softboard. It is made of a foamy material that doesn't hurt when it hits you on the head. Softboards are only for beginners, though, because once you learn how to ride, you'll want a board that is much more maneuverable.

Leash. A leash attaches the board to your ankle. This keeps the board from getting away from you after a wipeout.

Surf wax. The goal is to make your board smooth and slippery on the waves but not so slippery that you fall off. A good, well-applied coating of wax—and traction pads to keep your feet in place—is what does the trick.

Bathing suit/wet suit. Depending on how cold the water is, you'll surf in an ordinary bathing suit or in a specially designed neoprene wet suit. Most people think a wet suit keeps you warm. It doesn't—it just makes you less cold! Still, that's important, because too much time in cold water can dull your judgment and damage your health, even causing hypothermia.

Noseride. An old-style trick. When surfers rode longboards, they'd step forward to the very end of the board and stand there as they rushed in toward the beach. When you're so far forward that your toes are curling off the front of the board, that's "hanging ten."

Wipeout. When you go down. Watch out for your surfboard—it's probably falling *above* you, waiting to knock you on the head.

SURF SAFE
Surfing Etiquette and Rules

1 *Know the ocean.* Probably more than any other extreme sport, surfing happens in an unpredictable environment that can turn deadly. Good surfers know their limits, play it safe, and have a healthy understanding of the ocean's power.

2 *Show respect.* The better surfers always have priority over the beginners. That means some of them can be rude about showing it, but it's your job as a "grommet," or beginner, to know when you can "drop in" to a wave and when you need to hold back.

3 *The first person on the wave owns it.* If you cut somebody off after they've already taken a wave, you've committed a major surfing mistake. You'll probably hear about it, too. If you do it by accident, apologize and say it won't happen again. Never do it on purpose.

4 *Keep it clean.* The ocean and the beach are precious natural resources. Don't litter, and remember that fighting pollution gives surfers more—and better—places to surf.

HAWAIIAN SURFING WORDS

Hawaii is still the spiritual and literal home of the best surfers. It's a place every surfer dreams about visiting. Here are some Hawaiian words surfers use:

Aloha (ah-LOW-hah): Hello; love; goodbye

He'e nalu (heh-aye-NAH-loo): A surfer

Kahuna (kah-HOO-nah): A priest. The "Big Kahuna" means somebody who deserves respect.

Nalu (NAH-loo): Wave

Pae (pah-AYE): To ride a wave

Papa-he-nalu (pah-pah-hay-NAH-loo): Surfboard

Wahine (wah-HEE-nee): Woman surfer

Kelly Slater in 1997's Rip Curl Pro competition.

SURFING RESOURCES

Two magazines—*Surfer* and *Surfing*—cover the sport with the latest news, information about places to surf, and, most important, fantastic photography. Reading them is a great way to get inspired to actually go out and surf. *Wahine* is another surf magazine that's up-and-coming and, as the name suggests, is aimed toward women. The Surfrider Foundation can give you information on the important environmental issues—such as pollution, development, and erosion—that threaten surfing and ocean life in general. Contact Surfrider at 122 South El Camino Real, #67, San Clemente, CA 92672. The Surfrider website is at http://www.surfrider.org.

Skateboarding

Skateboarding is so much fun because it has so many variations. Looking for basic transportation? A skateboard can get you to school. Looking for competition? Head for the nearest ramp and you'll find all the talent you can handle. Skateboarding is about individual style. Some riders prefer to do their tricks on street corners, sliding and banging off anything they come up against. Others like to ride downhill on flexible, superlong boards that attain speeds of up to sixty miles per hour. There's even a form of mountain skateboarding where the boards have huge, knobby wheels for speeding downhill on dirt. And there's a whole culture that revolves around skateboarding, too. Besides riding, the sport's other components include fashion, art, photography, and music.

HOW SKATEBOARDING HAPPENED

Take a sidewalk scooter and remove the handle. Mix in a dash of surfing. Blend carefully with tons of kids growing up in the suburbs of California in the 1960s, looking for a way to get around. That's how skateboarding was invented.

In the 1950s and 1960s skateboarding was an underground sport. There were companies that made boards, but many riders

preferred to build their own out of planks and dismantled roller skates. These boards were fun, but they were harsh to ride—and sometimes pretty dangerous. The first big skateboarding boom petered out in the mid-1960s because technology hadn't caught up with the sport to make it easier and safer.

That happened in 1973 with the invention of the urethane wheel. Urethane is a soft, rubbery substance, and it did what the old clay or metal roller-skate wheels never could: It smoothed the ride. It allowed skateboarders to be limited only by their daring, not their equipment. It was during the 1970s that the basic foundation of today's skateboard world was formed. Tricks were invented—notably by Tony Alva and Jay Adams—and many of them took place in empty swimming pools, whose bowl-like sides were used by skaters to build speed and launch themselves into the air. The next step was ready-built skate parks, but these didn't last long. By 1979 the sport was once again slumping, and most of the parks closed.

Skateboarding has always gone in cycles, and nobody really knows why. One reason might have to do with the age of typical skateboarders. They're usually teenage boys (or at least they were in the old days). It was reasoned that once the current skate crowd grew up, it was a matter of chance if the next generation would catch the fever. Some did, some didn't.

In the 1980s skateboarding was about cities. Where 1970s riders preferred pools and parks, 1980s riders—including Tony Hawk, Steve Caballero, and Mark Gonzalez—didn't have the chance to ride in those places. So they made the street their park, from New York City's Brooklyn Banks to San Francisco's Embarcadero. This move to the streets led to many public restrictions on skateboarding, giving birth to skateboarders' famous motto, "Skateboarding is not a crime." The sport also came to be associated with other outlaw movements, especially punk rock. The sport divided into two basic schools, street and "vert" (short for vertical, which means tricks on ramps and other objects that get the rider up into the air).

In the 1990s the street scene still exists, but it is being transformed by a more laid-back groove. This can be seen in the kinds of equipment that are now popular: shorter boards, better for pavement pounding, are out; longer boards, which move smoothly and are perfect for a graceful, fluid riding style, are back in.

Skateboarding is becoming more accepted in the mainstream. The hard-edged styles that once signified the sport's rebellious attitude have become quite trendy, even for nonskaters. And the sport continues to boom and evolve, with new teams sponsored by skateboard manufacturers, and skateboard designers becoming recognized by major galleries as important artists, proving that skateboarding, probably more than any other extreme sport, isn't just a sport. It's an entire culture that many people are now part of.

GEAR FOR GRINDING

Your basic skateboard is made up of three parts: a deck, wheels, and trucks. You need to learn how to take care of your board, especially the wheels, which have precision bearings inside them. You'd be amazed how much faster, smoother, and safer you can roll with a well-maintained set of bearings.

The Basics

Decks. As wide and wild as the world. One skateboard collector, Todd Huber (who is starting a skate museum in Southern California), has over 1,500 decks—and he's just beginning. Skate decks are produced in limited editions by talented artists and designers, and the coolest, newest decks are always hot commodities. They are also almost always completely destroyed after just a few weeks of riding—

the street is a tough place. Decks also come in different lengths, shapes, and flexibilities. Longer, more flexible decks equal smoother rides but fewer tricks.

Wheels. You can pick wheels in different sizes and softnesses, which are measured by durometer rating (the higher the durometer rating, the harder the wheel). Wheel size is subject to fashion. In the late 1980s wheels below forty millimeters in diameter were popular. Today they're bigger. Bigger wheels give a smoother ride.

Trucks. This is the metal part that attaches the wheels to the deck. You can pick them in different widths; "proper width" means your wheels are about even with the edges of your deck. The trucks flex so the skateboard can turn.

Helmets and pads. In the 1980s vert skaters wore full helmets and elbow, knee, and wrist pads. Many street skaters preferred not to use them. But safety equipment is worth considering, because it can save your skin—not to mention your skull—when you inevitably crash. And since you're riding a device that has four wheels and no brakes, you *will* crash.

TRICKS, TERMS, AND TECHNIQUES

Skateboarding is a sport you can do your way. There are many different styles to choose from and places to ride. But the basics—whether you're freestyling, downhilling, riding in the street, or catching air on a ramp—are the same.

The Lingo

Ollie. The most important trick in the book. When you ollie, you're jumping the skateboard. If you want to do any other trick, you have to learn to ollie. A high ollie (say, two feet) is a simple and amazing thing of beauty to watch, and even better to do.

Kick turn. Did I say the ollie was more important? I take it back. The kick turn is just as essential, especially for vert skating. A kick turn is just what it sounds like: a simple, rapid change of direction, by "kicking" the board around. Tricksters do it at the top of the ramp.

Grind. When the trucks of your skateboard slide along an edge, like a curb or a park bench. There are many types of grind. The basic element of them all is that you're moving not with your wheels but sliding along the area between them.

Fakie. When you ride backward. Skateboarders either put their left foot on the front of the board ("normal") or on the back ("goofy-foot"). When you pivot the board around backward so that your back foot is now in the front and your body is facing in the opposite direction, you've "gone fakie." This is essential, because going fakie helps you transition from trick to trick.

Flip. If you're a skateboarder, you've probably tried this. If you aren't, but you've seen skateboarders at play, you've seen it. The board goes up in the air and flips around, and you land on it and keep going. There are many ways to flip a board, ranging from easy to hard.

CLOTHES AND FASHION

No mention of skateboarding would be complete without discussing what to wear when you skate. Many skate companies are now making bigger profits from selling clothes (often to nonskaters) than

Skateboarding fashion has become an important aspect of the sport.

boards. Why? Because skateboard clothes are comfortable and good-looking. Skateboarders are an individualistic bunch, and that makes them creative. Many have found an outlet for their creative energy in fashion. But remember: Wearing the clothes doesn't make you a skateboarder. Skating does.

SUPERSTARS AND SUPER PLACES

In skateboarding, people define the places that become famous, as opposed to surfing, where places empower the people. Here are some of skateboarding's most famous riders and the places they ride.

Super Skaters

Tony Hawk. The man who changed skating forever. Hawk grew up in San Diego, and he epitomized skateboarding in the mid-1980s, wearing clothes from Vision Street Wear, and doing his tricks while the punk rock was blaring. The amazing thing is that Hawk is still skating—and still winning. In 1997 he was the first person ever to cleanly land one of the sport's most difficult tricks, a 540-degree McTwist (a kind of midair front-to-back spin/flip).

Mark Gonzalez. "The Gonz"—a quiet, reclusive, and intense person, and an aggressive, unique skater—is the quintessential modern skate artist. Mark's work on skateboard decks has appeared in art galleries in New York and San Francisco, and now he's even painting on canvas.

Jaime Reyes. One of the world's best female skateboarders, Reyes is one of the few to make a living at it. She's from Hawaii, so she knows how to surf, too (even after thirty years the sports still have much in common), and she's sponsored by Real Skateboards. That's because she's the real deal!

Killer Places

The Embarcadero, San Francisco, California.

Once, the Embarcadero—a spot right on the water in downtown San Francisco—was the sport's most famous spot. Dozens of pros skated there, inspired by the fact that photographers from the biggest skateboard magazine, *Thrasher,* worked nearby and often

prowled around with their cameras. But if you go to the Embarcadero today, you'll find a strict "no skating" policy enforced. Don't worry: The San Francisco skate community can still be found just a mile away at Pier Seven.

The Brooklyn Banks, New York City, New York. Located just beyond City Hall in Manhattan, this is one of the prime locations for East Coast street skating. The skating here is aggressive, with lots of big ollies and nighttime sessions. The Banks are right beneath the Brooklyn Bridge, and skaters use the various architectural features of the area—the curbs, bridge pylons, and benches—to hone their skills. A few years ago a skater named Matthew Mento built a ramp here and tried to turn the Banks into an official skate park, but authorities destroyed it within a few hours.

Your ramp, Anywhere, U.S.A. Looking for a backyard project? Got no place to practice? Do what hungry skaters have been doing for years. Build your own ramp. It's not that hard or expensive and you might even be able to find a friendly park or schoolyard in your neighborhood to put it in. There are lots of ramp plans available—you can find ads for them in the back of most skateboard magazines or get them free on the Internet at http://www.heckler.com/ramps.html.

TO FIND OUT MORE

The best place to learn about skateboarding is at your local skateboard shop. There are also many skate magazines, the oldest of which are *Thrasher* and *Transworld Skateboarding*. If you want information about skateboards and skaters, you can also write to the biggest skate company on the planet, World Industries, at

815 North Nash, El Segundo, CA 90245, or call them at 1-800-500-5015. For information on competition, contact the California Amateur Skateboard League/Professional Skateboard League (CASL/PSL) at P.O. Box 30004, San Bernardino, CA 92413. Finally, for information about skate tours, camps, and competitions—as well as information on the sport's history, skate park locations, and equipment—visit the TumYeto website at http://www.skateboard.com.

In-Line Skating

I n-line skating is one of the most popular and fastest growing extreme sports. People do it on the street, in parks, on enclosed tracks, and at special facilities that have an assortment of ramps and obstacles similar to those found in skateboard parks. According to the in-line skate industry, over thirty million people in the United States now own a pair of in-line skates. In-line skating is also great exercise, so you can keep fit while you're getting thrills. What could be better?

HOW IN-LINE SKATING STARTED

You might call them Rollerblades®—many people do—since most people believe that the sport began with the invention of the Rollerblade in 1980. This is and isn't true. The Rollerblade company did make the in-line skate practical and popular, and it still sells more in-line skates than anybody else. But did you know that the in-line skate was really invented over three hundred years ago, in Holland?

In order to understand how this could be, you need to know more about what an in-line skate is. Like the once popular roller skate, it's a boot with wheels. But unlike a roller skate, the wheels are all in a straight row. Modern in-line skates have anywhere from three to five wheels. The straight-line configuration of the wheels is what gives in-line skates their speed and maneuverability, and what makes them a special favorite with ice-skaters, because they feel so much like ice skates when you're on them.

In fact, that's exactly what prompted the invention of in-line skates. A Dutch inventor wanted to enjoy the feeling of ice skates even in summer, so he attached wooden spools to his shoes, and away he went. Various others came up with similar designs throughout the eighteenth century.

Over a century later American James Plimpton invented the roller skate. His design gained instant popularity, featuring two sets of two side-by-side wheels. But while roller skates became popular, they didn't offer anything close to the sensation ice-skaters wanted.

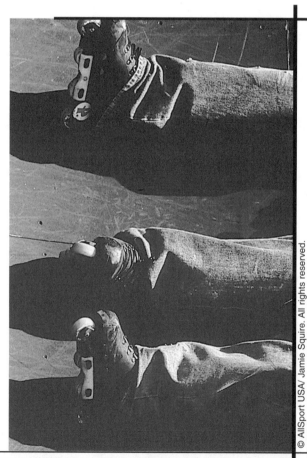

It took two brothers from Minneapolis, Scott and Brennan Olson, to come up with that feeling. Using an old Dutch skate as a model, they came up with the first modern in-line skate. They called it the "Rollerblade" and started selling them in 1980. As with skateboards, the advent of comfortable high-quality urethane wheels made possible new levels of performance.

Rollerblades were a huge hit. Why did they suddenly become so popular? Throughout the 1970s a roller-skating craze had washed over American cities, featuring disco dancing in parks and roller rinks. In the 1980s a fitness craze swept the country. The Rollerblade was the logical combination of the two. Also, in-line skates are perfect for cities. People who can't find a place to lock or store a bicycle can commute, have fun, and stay in shape with a product that takes up no more space than a pair of winter boots.

Today there are many varieties of in-line skates, costing from as little as $20 to over $500. Some skates even have built-in brakes and speedometers! In-line skating is recognized as a competitive sport as well as a culture. You'll find racers as fit and intense as any long-distance runner, and thrill-seekers as ready to take risks and do tricks as any skateboarder you know.

TRICKS, TERMS, AND TECHNIQUES

In-line skating is a lot like ice-skating. Unlike ice-skating, however, you can't cut a sharp edge into the ice to help you stop. Combine that with the fact that you're probably out on rough streets instead of a groomed rink and you'll understand why becoming good at in-line skating requires practice and finesse.

The Moves

Stopping. The number-one question beginners ask is "How do I stop?" Stopping isn't as hard as you might think. The trick is using the heel pad on your skate, and keeping your balance while you do it. A second method involves turning your rear skate perpendicular to the ground and dragging to a stop. Finally, there's the time-tested beginner's method: grabbing something or riding onto the grass!

Crossovers. A crossover is an essential technique that opens the door to nearly every other advanced in-line method or trick. It means going along a curve with a smooth, steady stroke, with the outer skate "crossing over" the inner. If you're still not clear on the concept, watch a hockey game. Notice the fluid way the players maneuver the sides of the rink. They're doing crossovers.

Backward. Going backward is an essential technique, and way cool. Most people get their first taste of going backward by accident—they begin to roll the wrong way down a hill! This is actually not a bad way to learn, as long as the hill's not too big! Finding a small, short incline and going down it will help you learn how to keep control even when you're going in the "wrong" direction. Ultimately, you work your way up to really propelling yourself backward. Combine backward skating with a crossover, and guess what: You're an expert.

Jumping. Many of the same tricks and terms found in skateboarding apply to in-line skating. "Catching air" on in-line skates is probably a little easier than on a skateboard. The major difference is that your skates are attached to your feet. Landings can be quite different. When a skateboarder lands, he or she has to end up on the board or bail out on foot. In-liners don't have that option. They always land on their wheels, which means that they have to know how to keep moving as soon as they hit the ground.

Down the stairs. This is something every in-line skater wants to try. It looks scary, but most folks who go down a flight of stairs on their skates find it easier than they thought. It does take practice, though, to do it well and safely. One important rule is to not panic. Stair-jumpers who hesitate at the last minute are more likely to crash. Anybody who wants to try stair-jumping should certainly be wearing a helmet, pads, and wrist guards.

Roller hockey. This is an exciting and relatively new development in the in-line world. It's just like ice hockey, but with a ball. There are organized teams and leagues, as well as informal street games (often played in a parking lot, using a couple of trash cans as goals). You don't need a whole team, either—just a few people and the right equipment: sticks, gloves, and helmets. It's also a great way to learn—fast—because the game doesn't give you a chance to slow down! Contact Roller Hockey International (see the listing on page 59) for more information.

THE GEAR

The most important thing you can own is a good pair of skates that fit well and are well taken care of. Most brands of in-line skates have models especially made for kids, which are good to learn on. As you get better, you'll develop your own taste for a particular brand or style.

Skate basics

How many wheels? Good question. Four wheels is the standard, and a four-wheel skate is a good skate for general use. Five wheels are often found on racing skates, which also have lower, less bootlike shoes and rarely have heel stoppers. Hockey skates

World In-line Championships, Venice, California.

usually have five wheels, also. Three wheels are mostly found on toy-store skates.

Laces and buckles. You'd be surprised, but a lot of skaters argue about what the best way is to get into your skates and secure them to your feet. Hockey skates have laces, but most skates have a combination of straps and buckles (as well as laces) that secure in the front, the back, or both. Buckles are nice because they're very quick and easy. Laces are simple and less expensive, but they're tougher to keep tight. Neither is a particular mark of a skate's quality. There are fine skates with buckles and fine ones with laces.

Are the inexpensive skates any good? A lot of people would say no. The problem with lower-priced skates is that they use wheels and bearings of poor quality. They may not fit comfortably or offer enough support for serious riding. But any pair of skates is better than none, and you *can* learn on budget skates. If you fall in love with the sport and want better gear, figuring out a way to save for them is definitely worthwhile. Another tip if you want really good skates: Buy used ones. Just make sure that all the straps and buckles are intact and that the wheels spin freely.

Caring for your bearings. As in skateboarding, bearing maintenance will keep your skates rolling smoothly. Most bearings come in cartridge form, so they can easily be replaced. Just pop out the old cartridge and put a new one in. You also need to rotate your wheels every month. Move the front ones to the middle, the middle ones to the back, and the back ones to the front. This will make sure that your wheels wear and roll evenly. If you're not sure how, ask someone who works in a store that sells skates, and they can explain it to you.

Skate brakes. Most in-line skates have a small heel pad that you press along the ground when you want to stop. There are also models that have more sophisticated brake mechanisms that actually force the heel pad downward when you slide your foot forward. This is good technology for folks who really feel like they can't learn to stop on their own, but most people *can* learn!

THE NINE BEST PLACES TO SKATE

Rollerblade came up with this list, based on a poll of its customers, of the best places to skate in the United States. These are also great places to learn, because you'll see dozens or even hundreds of other skaters, all out practicing. It's a great way to spend a family afternoon. (This list comes courtesy of Rollerblade. You can also add your favorite spot by visiting Rollerblade's website at http://www.rollerblade.com.)

1 *Central Park, New York City, New York.* You'll be joined by hundreds of other skaters, as well as bikers and joggers, with the skyscrapers of the Big Apple towering around you! On weekends, there's a slalom course set up on the west side of the park.

2 *Rock Creek Park, Washington, D.C.* There are two trails to choose from in the nation's capital. Beach Drive is closed to traffic on weekends for skaters to take the two-mile jaunt. For a longer ride, try the ten-mile Capital Crescent Trail, which starts in Georgetown, paralleling the Potomac River.

3 *The Lakes, Minneapolis, Minnesota.* Home of the Rollerblade, Minneapolis has over ten miles of lakeside paths. Start at the Lake Harriet Bandshell and work your way around Lake Calhoun and Lake of the Isles.

4 *Fairmount Park, Philadelphia, Pennsylvania.* This was home to the earliest roller-discoing, and the scene still lives, in-line style. West River Drive is closed to traffic on weekend mornings in the summer. The smooth, paved surface is ideal for beginning skaters and speedsters.

5 *Lake Front Path, Chicago, Illinois.* A marathon! This path is over eighteen miles long, but there are shorter sections, like the mile-long promenade at the Navy Pier. Bonus: There's also a Ferris wheel there!

6 *Boulder Creek Path, Boulder, Colorado.* There's so much to do and see along the six-mile-long Boulder Creek Path that you may find yourself taking numerous "side trips" along the way. A good starting point is at Tenth and Arapahoe, which will swing you right by the special Children's Fishing Pond.

7 *Golden Gate Park, San Francisco, California.* On Sundays, half of John F. Kennedy Drive is closed to traffic, and skaters can participate in roller-hockey games, veer down a slalom course, or hang around Sixth Avenue and Fulton Street, where there's music playing and freestyle skating and dancing. San Francisco also has a famous Friday Night Skate, where hundreds of skaters meet weekly at 8:00 P.M. at the Justin Herman Plaza, and finish their twelve-mile skate around 11:30 P.M.

8 *Veloway at Circle C, Austin, Texas.* This one belongs to skaters! Joggers and cars are not allowed on this three-mile paved loop through Austin's hill country. The Veloway is open seven days a week, and features slow and fast lanes for those who want to cruise and those who want to fly.

9 *The Strand, Pacific Palisades, California.* This two-lane path starts at the base of Pacific Palisades and goes through some of the most picturesque beaches on the West Coast. While skating all the way to Redondo Beach, you'll pass through Santa Monica, Marina del Rey, Venice Beach, and "Muscle Beach," as well as through the set of *Baywatch*! Who knows who you might see!

SKATING SAFE

In-line skating is a fun sport, but to stay safe you have to follow some simple rules. You should also be aware that, like skateboarders, in-line skaters can give the sport a negative image by being impolite or too wild in heavily crowded places. Save your tricks for your secret spot.

Protect Yourself

Helmets, always. Bike riders used to think helmets weren't cool. Today everybody wears one and nobody worries about what's hip. Bike helmet companies often make in-line skate helmets, and they're comfortable and good-looking. You need one.

Wrist guards. The most common in-line injury is falling down on your outstretched hands, resulting in painful wrist sprains or breaks. To avoid this, simple wrist guards—the same kind snowboarders use—are essential.

Knee pads. The second most common injury is less serious, but still painful: scraped knees. You don't want to mess with your knees, because bad knees can make skating difficult for a long time.

FOR MORE INFORMATION

For general in-line skating information, contact the International In-line Skating Association (IISA), 3720 Farragut Avenue, Suite 400, Kensington, MD 20895, (301) 942-9770. If you call them at 1-800-56-SKATE, they'll send you "Gear Up! Guide to In-line Skating." The price couldn't be better—it's free! The group's website is at http://www.iisa.org.

For information on roller hockey, contact Roller Hockey International, 5182 Katella Avenue, Suite 106, Los Alamitos, CA 90720, (310) 430-2423.

One of the best sources for information about in-line skating is at http://www.skatefaq.com, a website that has links to dozens of other great sites and has a comprehensive collection of questions and answers about the sport. You can also find nearly every in-line skate maker, most of them with comprehensive product catalogs and selection guides.

Snowboarding

In the world of board sports, snowboarding falls between surfing and skating, combining a little bit of both and ending up completely unique. It adds the thrill of skiing—moving fast on snow, through trees and across perfect, frosty terrain—but includes more tricks and smoother moves. There's nothing like blasting through the powder, and moving smoothly, almost like you're going through water, as the mountain sun warms your back.

HOW SNOWBOARDING HAPPENED

Though people have been riding down hills on single boards for years (there was a sport prior to snowboarding that didn't catch on called "snurfing"), the modern sport got its beginnings in the 1970s, when Jake Burton of Manchester, Vermont, began to make custom wooden snowboards. Burton used rubber straps to hold his winter boots on, and the sport was on its way. Though many people associate the sport with the West, snowboarding's history is more closely tied to Vermont. That's where the first national snowboard races were held and the first snowboard park—where boarders could practice their tricks without running into skiers—was created.

Snowboarding has evolved quite a bit since Jake Burton made the first boards in his garage. (Burton himself is now a major snowboard mogul and his company is the world's largest snowboard manufacturer.) Almost instantly snowboarders divided into two camps: Alpine riders, who prefer long runs down steep, groomed slopes; and freestylers, who like to do tricks in snowboard parks and on manicured "snow tubes" called half-pipes. The vast majority of snowboarders actually fit between the two extremes and are called freeriders.

Most equipment sold these days resembles freestyle gear more than it does Alpine. That means soft, walkable boots and shorter, fatter, more flexible boards. Alpine riders usually choose hard boots and longer, sleeker snowboards. The newest innovation in snowboarding is click-in bindings. It used to be that when you got off the ski lift, you'd have to sit down and spend a few minutes strapping your feet onto your board. The new bindings let you "stomp and romp." You just press your foot down and you're attached and ready to go.

One of the best things about snowboarding is that it attracts an equal number of boys and girls, kids and adults. Each rider can have his or her own style, and families can snowboard together. The snowboard parks—usually located at the bottom of a ski area, near the lodge—are prime hangouts for teenage snowboarders, who practice tricks, relax, and listen to music. Really extreme snowboarders avoid ski areas altogether, sometimes spending an entire day hiking up remote mountains in snowshoes in order to end it with one perfect run back to the lodge.

At first, snowboarders conflicted with skiers, who didn't understand how something so radically different than what they were used to could be allowed on the slopes. But the years have softened the relationship, and today about one-quarter of all lift tickets sold in the ski industry worldwide are bought by snowboarders.

TERMS, TRICKS, AND TECHNIQUES

Many snowboard tricks have the same names as their skateboard counterparts, and there's no doubt that knowing how to skateboard or surf makes learning to snowboard much easier. But each term changes a bit as it crosses to a new sport.

The Lingo

Air. When you "get air," you're flying. Nearly every snowboard trick involves air. Learning to get air means starting with small jumps and learning how to stay relaxed on the landing.

Grab. When you're getting air, and you grab the board. This is a trick in and of itself, but it is also the opening move (or a more complicated addition) to other tricks.

Gap jump. Just what it sounds like: snowboarding's most exciting trick, where a rider leaps across a huge gap. This is very hard and risky, but when the pros pull it off, it's one of the most exciting things you'll ever see.

McTwist. One of the best tricks on the half-pipe. The rider approaches the half-pipe wall, takes off, rotates toward the "backside" (the side of the board where the heels are placed) while flipping frontward. A perfect landing keeps your forward momentum.

Powder. Good, fresh powder is like water—so light you'd sink into it if you stopped. Good powder riders keep their speed up and float above the fluff. Many people feel deep, fresh powder is the ultimate snowboarding pleasure.

Boardercross. This is one of the coolest snowboard activities. It's kind of an obstacle course, where racers compete against other snowboarders head-to-head, over jumps, banked turns, and other man-made elements.

Rotation. Rotation is what you do when you're in the air. The more rotations, the harder the trick. You can rotate either sideways (a twist) or head-over-foot (a flip). There are degrees of rotation: A 180 is a half-circle; a 720 is two full circles (360 and 540 come in between).

THE GEAR

Snowboard equipment comes in many styles and colors. Good outfits can be bought for as little as $300, and for as much as $1,000. If you're buying equipment, most ski areas will let you rent (or "demo") the gear you want before you buy, for the cost of a rental.

What You Need

Board. Boards come in various widths and shapes. The boards most preferred by freestylers are "dual tip," which means they have the same shape at both ends, so you can ride in either direction (riding in the opposite direction is called "going fakie," just like in skateboarding). Alpine boards—used for carving tight, fast turns—have a single tip and a tail, which helps them cut through the snow quicker. Another factor is board length. A good rule of thumb is that, when held upright, the board should extend from the floor to somewhere between your chin and the bottom of your neck. The shorter the board, the better it is for tricks. Longer boards are better for carving.

Boots. The more flexible the boot, the easier it is to do tricks, but the harder it is to carve. Most riders, not surprisingly, prefer a boot that's somewhere in between the two extremes. Snowboard boots are usually quite comfortable, and newer models are superlight, too, so you can wear them all day without feeling like your feet are made of lead.

Bindings. With standard bindings you just strap your feet in and go. Newer systems are click-in, requiring a special "cleat" on the bottom of your boot that mates with the binding, which is attached to the board. Click-in bindings are faster and more convenient, but they're also more complicated and, in some cases, offer less support to the back of your ankle, making them less suitable for power carving and tricks.

Clothes. Snowboard clothes are becoming as fashionable as skateboard clothes. Lots of people who never rode a snowboard in their life are choosing snowboard clothes as winter streetwear. They're also more expensive, because true snowboard garb is quite technical. If you're intimidated by the selection, just remember that the one thing you must have is a pair of waterproof pants to keep you dry after you fall. The fancy jackets, hats, and the rest can wait.

Goggles. Good eyewear is another essential, though there's some debate over whether this means glasses or goggles. In either case, you want quality. Eyewear should be shatterproof and should filter out ultraviolet rays (look for lenses that say "100% UV protection"). Lens color is especially important: In the middle of the afternoon on overcast days, the terrain gets "flat," and snowboarders can have a hard time reading the bumps and lumps. The proper shade of lens can help increase contrast and safety.

Gloves. Don't skimp on these, either. You need good gloves both to protect your hands and keep them warm. Mittens are acceptable,

too. One new innovation in gloves are ones with built-in wrist guards. They're great. If you go the old-fashioned route, with wrist protectors that are separate from your gloves, make sure you try the gloves on while you're wearing the protectors.

SUPERSTARS AND SUPER PLACES

Here are the people and locations that snowboarding has immortalized.

Hot Boarders

Shaun Palmer. Probably the sport's most extreme character, Shaun Palmer is equally at home on a mountain bike or motorcycle as he is on a board. That's saying a lot, because Palmer is one of the most decorated snowboarders in history, taking nearly every event in every category at least once in his career, which began in 1985 and is still going strong.

Julie Zell. Julie may be one of the most daring snowboarders on earth. She's a three-time winner of the Queen of the Hill competition in Alaska, regarded as the world's most demanding board event. Zell's favorite terrain is deep in the backcountry, where waves of fluff sit untouched by humans.

Killer Slopes

Snowbird, Utah. *Snowboard Life* magazine named Snowbird the best place to ride in the country. The "'Bird" benefits from storms that blow up Little Cottonwood Canyon and wring themselves out on Snowbird and Alta, the nearby ski area that doesn't allow snowboarders. The mountain gets an amazing 450 inches of fluffy powder a year!

Stowe, Vermont. Stowe is a formidable mountain, and it was one of the first to welcome snowboarders. There's a reason Jake Burton moved to the area and made Stowe his testing ground. The "Front Four" are Stowe's hardest trails; the Lower Lord Snowboard Park is one of the newest in the East.

Squaw Valley North, Lake Tahoe, California. Probably the most "pro friendly" snowboard area in the continental United States. It's a favorite place for photographers and videomakers to shoot pros doing tricks. Legendary trails include KT22 and Granite Chief.

Mt. Baker, Washington. Simple and unpretentious, Baker hosts a famous annual slalom race and gets more snowfall than any other mountain in America: an average of 595 inches a year.

SAFETY TIPS

The first rule is take a lesson. Better yet, take five lessons. A good teacher can show you more—and get you started faster—than anyone else. Every snowboard area offers lessons for kids and grown-ups, individuals and groups. Many offer discount beginner packages that include lessons, lift tickets, and rentals for one low price.

Snowboarding can be hazardous. You never know what the conditions might be like at a ski area, and you can start moving very quickly very fast. You also have other snowboarders and skiers to look out for. You should know the skier's responsibility code, developed by ski areas and the ski industry, which also applies to snowboarders:

1 You must remain in control and proceed in such a manner that you can stop or avoid other people or objects.

2 As you proceed downhill or overtake another skier, you must avoid the persons below and beside you.

3 Do not stop where you obstruct a trail or are not visible from above.

4 When entering a trail or starting downhill, look uphill and yield to others.

5 If you are involved in or witness a collision, you must remain at the scene and identify yourself to the Ski Patrol.

6 You must use proper devices to prevent runaway equipment.

7 You must not use lifts or terrain if your ability is impaired through use of alcohol or drugs.

8 You must keep off closed trails and observe and obey all signs and warnings.

Other Tips

The most important thing to do is to stay within your level of skill. Most accidents happen when riders enter terrain that they're not familiar with or can't handle. Special caution is needed when snowboarding among trees. Besides the danger of hitting one, there are often large "sinkholes" of melted snow around tree trunks that riders can get stuck in. Tree riders, especially, should wear helmets.

SNOLYMPICS

Snowboarding was just added to the Olympics in 1998. Of the twelve-member U.S. team, Shannon Dunn (of Steamboat Springs, Colorado) and Ross Powers (of South Londonderry, Vermont) won medals. Want to earn your own spot on the team? Learn how by visiting the team's website at http://www.usskiteam.com/u/usskiteam/new/Snowboard.html, or by calling 1-800-950-USSA.

TO LEARN MORE

The two most popular snowboard magazines are *Transworld Snowboarding* and *Snowboarder*. Both are full of action pictures, hints on technique, and equipment reviews. If you're really serious about snowboarding, you should go to a snowboard school. You'll find advertisements for schools in the back of most snowboard magazines. Most schools last about a week and can help you improve a lot. Good snowboard sites on the Internet include Snowboarding On-line (www.snowboard.com) and TWSnow On-line (www.twsnow.com).

BMXing

Looking for the thrill of competition and the perfect combination of the tricks found in skateboarding and the speed and toughness of mountain biking? You've found BMX! BMX is centered around racing, on tracks all around the country. Many more riders have fun with freestyle, which concentrates on tricks and ramp action. The world of BMX is exploding right now. Dozens of new companies are springing up to manufacture cool, innovative twenty-inch wheel bikes. And more and more people—even grown-ups!—are discovering the fun of riding and playing on these light, cool, and highly maneuverable machines.

HOW BMX HAPPENED

Have you ever sat on your bike and pretended that it was a motorcycle? That's how BMX (short for "bicycle motocross") got started in the early 1970s. A group of California kids saw a documentary movie called *On Any Sunday,* which featured the adventures of Mert Lawill, one of the world's greatest motorcycle racers. In the movie Lawill jumped, throttled, and twisted his motorcycle up and over a circular motocross track, sending plumes of dust spewing through the air. When they saw it, the kids took their own bikes, set up tracks, and imitated the racers.

Today BMX is one of the most popular sports for kids all around the world. Two organizations hold races, and there are hundreds of local tracks. In addition, BMX has given birth to another sport: freestyle. Freestyle uses similar bikes but concentrates on tricks and action on ramps, similar to the ones used in skateboarding. In fact, since BMX bikes are so much lighter than the motorcycles they were originally built to imitate, the tricks you can do on them are really high-flying. Getting air on a BMX bike is bigger and badder than in just about any other extreme sport.

Unlike skateboarding or snowboarding, BMX has been very tightly organized almost from the beginning. The National Bicycle League (NBL), founded in 1974, was the first group to unify state and local BMX organizations. Today the NBL sanctions over three thousand races per year, including twenty-three national events and twelve regional ones. The NBL was quickly followed by the American Bicycle Association (ABA). Both are big, and the NBL has more members in the eastern United States, while the ABA is larger on the West Coast.

A typical BMX race starting line.

In recent years, the nonracing part of BMX—freestyle and its cousins—has become as popular as racing. There are many kinds of freestyle, and all of them are about self-expression. The long-time king of this aspect of the sport is Oklahoma's Matt Hoffman, who invented or perfected nearly every well-known freestyle trick.

ALL ABOUT BMX RACING

If you're interested in BMX, you'll be interested in racing. Here's how it works at ABA races. NBL races are similar, only you need a different license to participate. (Each group requires that you get a license, which provides insurance and local track information. Since the two leagues aren't affiliated, one license isn't good at the other's events.)

ABA Races

The track. The first thing you'll see is a dirt track, averaging about one thousand feet long. The track snakes and spirals over and around itself, and there are plenty of jumps and banked turns. There will be riders practicing, too, and some of them will be really good! You'll be amazed at how high they can jump and how graceful their landings are.

The race. A BMX race usually lasts under a minute. That means you have to start fast, because it's over before you know it. The starting area is filled with excitement and anticipation. You'll notice that some riders get an extra edge at the start by balancing the bike with both feet on the pedals (the correct term for this is a "track stand"). When the starting gun goes off, these racers have the ability to burst forward just a little faster.

Getting Better

You're going to wonder how the pros get so much air and land so smoothly. The answer is practicing! Most BMX tracks have a "practice night" where anyone can show up and hone his or her skills. And there are a lot of homemade practice areas, too, usually in vacant lots or fields.

Where Did the Name Come From?

One thing people often ask about BMX is why the last letter in the abbreviation is X—after all, the term is "bicycle motocross." Though some folks joke that the X stands for "Xmas" (because everybody wants a new bike under the tree), the truth is that nobody knows. The X just sounds cool.

THE FAMILY OF BMX

As with skateboarding, there's street freestyle and ramp-oriented freestyle. But in BMX, they break down into even more categories. Here's what's what.

BMX Categories

Freestyle. Pure and simple, riding your bike and doing tricks. Typical freestyle bikes have front forks that can spin around, and pegs on the back wheels so riders can stand on them.

Ramp riding. Just what it sounds like. Ramp riders do their thing on half-pipes and quarter-pipes, curved wooden platforms that help build momentum and launch the rider into the air.

Dirt jumping. Probably the purest form of the sport, because it's so close to what riders do in their own backyards. Start with a big pile of dirt, fly off it, and land safely. Do tricks while you're airborne.

Matt Hoffman. Photo by Brad McDonald.

Flatland. Riding without jumping. Flatlanders do a lot of hopping and spinning on their bikes, but they don't launch themselves.

TRICKS AND TECHNIQUES

While BMXing may seem a lot like mountain biking, it actually has its own set of tricks and jumps.

The Lingo

Back-flip. Jump into the air, spin around once, and stick the landing. One of the most crowd-pleasing "vert" BMX techniques.

720. As in snowboarding, a 720 is two full horizontal rotations.

Truck driver. A 360—a single full horizontal rotation—while spinning the handlebar around, like the steering wheel of a truck.

Bunny hop. Same as in mountain biking but easier, because the bike's so much lighter. Hopping the bike up into the air.

Endo. Also called a "nose wheelie." It's when you balance on the front wheel of your bike instead of the back.

BMX SUPERSTARS

Here are the names you should know in the world of BMX and freestyle.

Extreme BMXers

Matt Hoffman. Now the owner of Hoffman Bicycles, Matt virtually reinvented the sport in the 1990s with a combination of daring and poise. His greatest trick? Probably being towed through a quarter-pipe on a motorcycle, so he could get more speed than his legs could generate!

Dave Mirra. A freestyler who rides for Haro, Mirra is known as one of the smoothest, most technically skilled riders around.

John Purse. One of the most consistent winners in BMX racing, Purse is known for his strength, his jumping ability, and his speed in the straightaways.

T.J. Lavin. Winner of the X Games (see chapter 11), T.J. gets more air than anyone. How does he do it? By practicing on a trampoline with a bike that has no wheels.

FEEL GOOD, RIDE SAFE

Here is the official ABA recommendation on making sure your bike and body are safe and well protected:

Your Bike

1 Make sure all bolts are tight, especially axle bolts and stem bolts.

2 All reflectors must be removed to keep them from breaking or harming other competitors. If you plan on riding your BMX bike on the street, though, you *must* put your reflectors back on.

3 If your bike has a kickstand, it must be taken off.

4 Your bike needs the three required pads: the one that covers the crossbar of your handlebars; the one that covers

Matt Hoffman. Photo by Brad McDonald.

the handlebar stem; and the one that covers the top tube of the frame.

5 You need a number plate. Usually you get one when you sign up for a race. If not, a heavyweight paper plate makes a good substitute.

Yourself

There's a wide assortment of BMX clothes out there, and most look really cool. But you don't need the full-on outfit to get started, according to the ABA. Jeans and a T-shirt are just fine. Here's the ABA suggested clothing list:

1 Long-sleeve shirt

2 Long pants

3 Helmet (Loaner helmets are available at some tracks.)

4 Ordinary pair of tennis shoes

OTHER IMPORTANT THINGS TO KNOW

Be prepared! When you find your local track, make sure you get proper directions and get there on time. Also, find out what the entry fees are. If you want to learn more, many tracks hold beginner clinics that will fill you in on all the basics.

CAMPS AND CLINICS

There are two very popular BMX camps where you can go for a week or longer to sharpen your skills.

Richie Anderson is a two-time national number-one-ranked rider and member of the BMX Hall of Fame. His camp number is (805) 272-1404.

Greg Hill's Speed Seminars are another camp with very flexible program schedules and a large variety of options. Call (818) 951-0051.

FOR MORE INFORMATION

American Bicycle Association ABA

The ABA website is at http://www.ababmx.com. They also publish *BMXer* magazine. Find out about both by writing to: ABA, P.O. Box 718, Chandler, AZ 85244

National Bicycle League NBL

3958 Brown Park Drive, Suite D

Hilliard, Ohio 43026

The NBL website is at http://www.nbl.org. The NBL can also tell you about a track near you. Call 1-800-886-2691 and they'll send you a postcard listing nearby BMX resources.

Magazines

RIDE, dedicated to freestyle, and *SNAP*, a BMX racing magazine, are both published by Ride Publishing at 1530 Brookhollow, Suite A, Santa Ana, CA 92705. Both contain the latest news, hot photos, and information on choosing the proper equipment.

Mountain Biking

Mountain biking is an awesome and challenging sport. What's so great about it? It isn't just that mountain bikes represent some of the coolest and most innovative technology this side of the space shuttle. It isn't just that mountain biking is now an official Olympic sport. No, the coolest thing about riding a mountain bike is that it's something anyone can do! Nearly everyone can already ride a bike, and if you can ride a regular bicycle, you can ride a mountain bike. The mountain bike is more than just a toy but is also a tool for exploring hills, valleys, and trails around your neighborhood and around the world.

HOW MOUNTAIN BIKES HAPPENED

Today over sixty million people in the United States own mountain bikes, and the sport is growing by leaps and bounds. It wasn't always that way. In fact, only twenty years ago the idea that somebody would equip a bike with fat tires and low gears to ride off-road was considered more than just a little extreme!

But in Marin County, north of San Francisco, a group of dedicated riders were doing just that. Gary Fisher, Charlie Kelly, and Joe Breeze were taking old bikes called "clunkers," most of which were built in the 1940s, and modifying them by adding brakes and

additional gears. They rode these bikes every weekend to the top of Mt. Tamalpais and then raced down.

Pretty soon, spectators started asking whether they could buy a clunker. The three pioneers were suddenly entrepreneurs. They called their creation the "Mountain Bike." Eventually, people from places as far away as New England heard about this new machine that was perfect for exploring the steep and rocky trails that were previously accessible only by foot or mountain goat. Several companies started building mountain bikes (the term eventually became generic), and by 1988 the boom had began. Mountain bikes were everywhere.

There are all kinds of ways to enjoy mountain biking. From the beginning, people have competed in races against each other. Racing serves another important purpose, too: Bike companies use the racers to test out new innovations that will ultimately make their way onto the ordinary bikes people buy from their local bike shops. But mountain biking isn't just about racing. People use their bikes to travel the world, spend time with their families, explore nature, or just have a little fun after school or on the weekend.

From its simple beginnings, mountain biking has become very sophisticated. Computers that were developed to build airplanes and spacecraft now design and manufacture mountain-bike parts; many former aerospace engineers now work in the bike industry. That two-wheeled fun machine is actually a wonder of science! Today mountain bikes are evolving even further. Companies are making bikes that look more like rockets, or motorcycles, which have front and rear suspension, for faster, safer handling and internal gears and disk brakes that work in the harshest conditions. Although some mountain bikes can cost as much as $5,000, you don't need to spend much at all to enjoy the sport. Even the most basic bike can travel the backcountry with safety, fun, and convenience.

TRICKS AND TECHNIQUES

The greatest thing about mountain biking is that nearly everybody can do it. The basic skills of bike riding—pedaling, braking, and turning—are well known to mostly everybody. But when you get into the dirt, there are some key tricks and techniques that help riders have more fun and handle almost any kind of terrain.

The Basics

Wheelie. This is one of the oldest bike tricks, one of the most fun, and one of the easiest. A wheelie involves simply lifting the front end of the bike and balancing on the back wheel as the bike moves forward. It isn't just a trick, either: Doing a mini-wheelie—over a rock, tree stump, or log—helps keep a rider rolling ahead on difficult trails.

Bunny hop. Think of the bunny hop as a "wheelie-plus." At first it looks like a wheelie, but then the rider pulls up on his or her back wheel to get the bike completely airborne. Bunny hops can be done standing in place (trials riders—bikers who specialize in tricks—use this to lift their bikes onto obstacles along a predetermined course), or while in motion. A full-speed bunny hop can actually make riding safer, since the bike is lifted *over* obstacles instead of riding into them.

Singletrack. "Singletrack" is a simple mountain bike term for a narrow, technical trail with lots of obstacles. Most mountain bikers consider riding singletrack to be the most exciting element of the sport—it's fun to swoop between the trees! But singletrack does require caution. Besides watching out for stumps, logs, and rocks, riders need to remember that there may be other people on the trail—hikers, horseback riders, kids, and other bikers. That means speed has to be tempered with courtesy.

Downhilling.

Downhill mountain-bike riding is becoming more and more popular. Many riders are now visiting ski areas in the summertime and taking chairlifts to the top for a fast-paced thrill ride to the bottom. Downhilling requires high skill and specialized equipment, including a bike with front and rear suspension and disk brakes, along with body armor (padding) and a full-face helmet.

Cross-country. Cross-country is the most common type of riding. It combines pavement and dirt, singletrack with downhill, narrow trails and wide ones, and everything in between. Cross-country riding also usually includes quite a bit of hillclimbing—which means riders have to be in shape! Hill climbing can hurt at first, but the reward of getting to the top of a hill is riding down it!

THE GEAR

Your Basic Mountain Bike

Fat tires alone don't necessarily make a real mountain bike. A real off-road bike has low gears, good brakes, and a front shock absorber. Most bikes from department and toy stores don't cut it. They usually don't have sufficient shock absorbers or safe brakes. Besides, a visit to a real bike shop can be fun, because that's where the real riders hang out!

Gears Without Tears

For years mountain-bike designers have been trying to make gears easier to shift. Today's shifting systems usually have twenty-one to twenty-four speeds, and use either a pair of push buttons on either side of the handlebars or a twist-grip system that looks like a motorcycle throttle. Either way, shifting is something that seems intimidating but actually takes just a few minutes to learn. The easiest way to figure it out is to experiment with the gears, testing to see what makes pedaling easier and harder. Use your ears—when something's grinding, you're probably not shifting smoothly. Some grinding sounds are to be expected—don't worry: The gears won't break!

Titanium and Miracle Metals

Bikes these days are made from many different materials. Aluminum is probably the most popular. Most bike components and many frames are made from this material, because it is lightweight, strong, and inexpensive. High-end bikes are often made of titanium, a rare metal that is even lighter and stronger than aluminum. Lower-end or cheaper bikes are often made from steel, though there are forms of steel tubing that are every bit as rare and high-tech as titanium. Finally composite materials (carbon fiber or thermoplastics) allow builders to depart from standard designs and create machines that look like they're from outer space—and ride like it, too!

SUPERSTARS AND SUPER PLACES

Mountain biking has both legendary people and legendary places. Each is usually special for a particular reason. There are places known for their riding fun, or extreme difficulty; there are famous downhillers as well as cross-country riders.

Killer Biking

Mammoth Mountain, California. This ski area in the California Sierra holds a famous race and bike festival every summer, often attracting as many as ten thousand spectators and riders. The highlight of Mammoth is the downhill Kamikaze, a two-mile race in which riders often reach speeds as high as sixty miles per hour!

24 Hours of Canaan, West Virginia. One of the most famous and difficult mountain bike events is the 24 Hours of Canaan, a full-day race that takes place in the mountains of West Virginia. The terrain is incredibly rocky and challenging, and riders struggle right through the night, often in temperatures below freezing, to complete the event.

John Tomac

Awesome Bikers

John Tomac. For more than ten years, John Tomac has been the Michael Jordan of mountain-bike racing. Tomac is one of the few racers who is equally good at cross-country and downhill. He also has been a professional road-bike racer. Tomac got his start as a teenage BMX competitor in Michigan, and went on to off-road fame and fortune.

Missy Giove. Giove is one of the sport's most exciting characters. Her nickname is "The Missile," because she's fast—faster than almost any other downhill racer, man or woman. Missy has a special way of talking (almost as fast as she rides!) that reflects her distinctive style and the electrically charged nature of the sport.

Susan DeMattei. Susan always has a smile and a kind word for her fans. All that friendliness paid off in 1996, when thousands cheered her on to win a bronze medal in the Olympics. Most people in the bike world thought it couldn't have happened to a nicer person—and most people were glad they didn't have to compete against her, because DeMattei is as tough as she is friendly!

FEEL GOOD, RIDE SAFE

Mountain biking is fun, but it can be dangerous if riders aren't careful. Following a few simple precautions makes mountain biking fun *and* safe.

Rules of the road

Helmets are cool. Everybody should wear a helmet. All the racers do, and it's rare to see anyone on the trail without one. Today's helmets are sleek, lightweight, and safe. One thing to remember: In order to do its job, a helmet has to fit properly, which means snug enough that it doesn't move around on your head. The best helmets are safety-certified by the Snell Memorial Foundation, and have a sticker inside that says so.

The right clothing. Biking in jeans and a T-shirt is fun, but most riders prefer to use specialty bike clothes. Why? Because padded gloves and shorts help prevent fatigue and soreness of the muscles and skin. Jerseys made of high-tech fabrics like Lycra help keep riders cool during long rides. Shatterproof sunglasses are important, too, protecting the eyes not only from the damaging rays of the sun but also from stray branches.

Working equipment. A good bike needs to be kept in proper condition for safe riding. That means making sure the brake pads aren't worn down, the wheels are running securely and straight, and that the cables and chains are in good condition. It isn't just safety, either: Who wants to walk home because their bike broke?

Being seen. Many riders visit their favorite trails at night—an experience that's exciting but also potentially dangerous. Luckily, night riding is made easier by the availability of powerful lights. Developed for the 24 Hours of Canaan race and adapted for general use, these lights illuminate the trails. They also help riders be seen by cars when they're riding on city streets.

IMBA's Rules of the Trail

1. Ride on open trails only.
2. Leave no trace on the trail.
3. Control your bicycle.
4. Always yield the trail to others.
5. Never spook animals.
6. Plan your route ahead and be ready for emergencies.

Cleaning your bike is an important part of keeping it working properly.

TO FIND OUT MORE

There are many organizations that provide information about mountain biking. The International Mountain Bike Association (IMBA) is devoted to helping riders learn to ride safely and in a way that's environmentally friendly. IMBA has even developed its own "Rules of the Trail" that it recommends everyone follow. IMBA also coordinates activities from local clubs, and can put you in touch with a mountain-bike group in your area.

International Mountain Bicycling Association

P.O. Box 7578
Boulder, CO 80306
Phone: (303) 545-9011
Fax: (303) 545-9026
E-mail: imba@aol.com

The National Off-Road Bicycle Association (NORBA) handles racing and competition. In order to race, riders pay a small fee to purchase a NORBA racing license. Norba is part of the Union Cycliste International (UCI), the worldwide group that sanctions bike racing. Both NORBA and the UCI can be contacted at:

One Olympic Plaza
Colorado Springs, CO 80909
Phone: (719) 578-4717
Fax: (719) 578-4596

There are lots of mountain-bike magazines. Two of the best are *Mountain Bike*, published by Rodale Press, which focuses on the latest equipment, techniques, and racing news, and *Bike*, published by Surfer Publications, which concentrates on adventure and high-quality photography.

The X Games and Even More Extreme Sports 11

THE X GAMES

Here's a secret: When the X Games were first invented by sports television network ESPN, most people in the extreme sports world didn't think much of it. The events seemed too programmed, and the sponsors didn't really seem to understand the sports.

That was then. This is now. Today the X Games—both the winter and summer versions—are one of the most popular sporting events in the world, both with fans and with the athletes.

Why the change? First of all, ESPN eliminated silly sports, like bungee jumping. Second, ESPN listened to what the athletes wanted and made the games a true test of physical and mental stamina. Third, there's nothing more exciting to watch than sports where people are participating mostly for love, not money, and playing their hearts out.

But there's another thing: Most of us look at the X Games and remember the times we were out mountain biking, or snowboarding, or skateboarding. So we can say: "Hey, that's like what I do!" Many people can't say that when it comes to football or basketball.

1997 Summer X Games.

How popular are they? In 1997 over two hundred thousand people watched the summer X Games in Oceanside, California. Just as they do in the Olympics, cities around the world are now bidding for the right to host the X Games.

One special X Games participant is April Lawyer. She's the only person to compete as both a mountain biker and a snowboarder. "It's really turned out to be a very cool thing," she says.

The future of the X Games is wide open, with more and more events being added and the definition of "extreme" constantly changing. One big question is, What happens when X-Game sports get added to the Olympics? In snowboarding the two peacefully co-exist. But mountain biking—at least in its traditional form—doesn't look like it will be a part of future X-Game competitions (though downhill and snow biking, which aren't in the Olympics, will remain in place).

Want to find out more about the X Games? There's usually information about it on ESPN and it's companion network, ESPN2. There are also extensive archives of X-Games information at the ESPN website: http://www.espn.com.

OTHER COMPETITIONS AND FESTIVALS

Each sport has its own national competitive series. You can find out about these in each sport's section in this book, or by reading the magazines dedicated to the individual sports. One skateboard/BMX event worth mentioning is the Warped Tour, sponsored by *Warp* magazine. This isn't really a competition as much as it is a festival: bands, fans, and pros all get together for a weekend of partying and showing off. You can learn more about the Warped Tour in the pages of *Warp*.

OTHER EXTREME SPORTS

New extreme sports are being invented every day, but there are sometimes arguments about whether or not a sport is really extreme. Here are the activities that are considered to be part of the extreme sports world right now.

More Extreme!

Adventure racing. This is as close as the extreme world gets to a team sport. A group of athletes, usually trained in different disciplines, compete in a point-to-point, multiday event that often includes rafting, kayaking, biking, running, and climbing.

Snow biking.

Barefoot waterskiing. You've seen waterskiing. The extreme version is just what it sounds like: doing it without a water ski! It requires a lot of skill and finesse.

Bodysurfing. You may have done this at the beach, but extreme bodysurfing is done in the really big waves—it's man (or woman) against the ocean, with no equipment.

Boogie boarding. Once considered unimportant by the surf community, boogie boarders (or body boarders) now have their own sport that's very separate from surfing. The key to boogie boarding is rolling and doing tricks with the board while you're in the water.

Extreme skiing. This used to be called "freestyle," and it's basically tricks-on-skis.

Rock climbing. This is one of the most physically demanding of the extreme sports, and it's probably as old as surfing. There are many types of rock climbing, too, ranging from controlled competition on artificial walls to no-safety-equipment free climbing in the wilderness.

Sky surfing. They drop you out of an airplane on what looks like a snowboard and you do tricks as you float down, before eventually releasing your parachute.

Snow biking. Officially invented by the X Games, it was bound to happen: riding down a ski slope on a bike. Snow biking is April Lawyer's specialty.

Street luge. A luge is a tiny platform that a rider lies down on and then hurtles

Street luge.

feet-first downhill, like a bullet. This is usually done on snow. Street luge does it on pavement. Imagine laying on your skateboard and going down the biggest hill in your neighborhood.

Telemark skiing. This is a combination of downhill and cross-country skiing, but it's done very aggressively. The skier's heel is free, so the skier can go wherever he or she wants in the backcountry, with no lifts required. Then, on the downhills, the heel can be fixed in place for high-speed action.

Windsurfing. People who didn't live near the ocean wanted to surf, but they had no ocean waves, so they attached sails to surfboards and invented this sport.

Wakeboarding. This is something like snowboarding on the water. A wakeboarder gets towed behind a boat at high speed, and then criss-crosses the boat's wake (the waves the boat makes as it turns) and does jumps and tricks on them. The wake becomes an instant liquid half-pipe.

Windsurfing.

Extreme Entertainment 12

 he following is a list of the best of the best in extreme sports books, movies, and video games.

BOOKS

Fat Tire: A Celebration of the Mountain Bike, by Amici Designs. Published by Chronicle Books—a complete, glossy history of the off-road lifestyle, filled with information about people, places, and products. (P.S., I co-wrote this book.)

Stoked: A History of Surf Culture. A glossy coffee-table volume by Drew Kampion, one of surfing's best-known journalists. This book perfectly captures surfing spirit and values. Maybe the best surf book ever published. From General Publishing Group.

Skateboarding: The Extreme, by Bill Gutman. This is a basic—and well-done introduction to the sport, not really a how-to—more of an encyclopedia. Published by St. Martin's Press.

Sick: A Cultural History of Snowboarding, by Susanna Howe, published by St. Martin's Press. Susanna spent a year living the snowboard life—riding, hanging out with other boarders, getting better, and keeping a cool action journal that tells all about it and the people she met.

BMX Bicycles, by Barbara Knox. A good basic book outlining the what-to-dos and how-to-do-thems of BMX. Published by Children's Press.

Wheel Excitement: The Official Rollerblade Guide to In-line Skating, by Neil Feineman. Neil Feineman is one of the best experts out there on in-line skating, and this book is essential for skaters of all levels. Published by Hearst Books.

VIDEOS

One of the best sources for extreme sports videos is the Surf Video Network—which sells videos for all action sports. Here are six of SVN's top sellers (you can contact the network by calling 1-800-822-0522; or visit their website at http://www.surfvideo.net):

Quicksilver: Kelly Slater and Lisa Anderson, and dozens of the world's top surfers, waves, and beaches. High-quality images shot on film, so it looks like a real movie. Produced by Quicksilver.

Rising: This skateboard video features over fifty skaters doing nearly every trick in the book. Ultra fast-paced and technical. Produced by World Market.

Inside Edge: This how-to in-line video features street action, shot on Venice Beach, California, with some of the best international instructors in the sport. Produced by Chilli Video.

Slanted and Enchanted: This snowboard video won the "Best of Snow" competition at the Gravity Sports Film Festival. That means it rules. Produced by Noyes Productions.

Matt Hoffman Headfirst: Falling clearly into the "I can't believe he did that" category, this BMX video features Matt Hoffman doing the impossible. Possibly the most exciting video ever. No joke. Produced by Head First.

Bragging Rights: The newest off-road cycling video from Taylor Congdon, this tape features Shaun Palmer and his yokel pals performing feats of dirt daring. Produced by Taylor Congdon.

VIDEO GAMES

2EXTREME. This is an all-in-one Playstation game that features in-line, mountain biking, skateboarding, and snowboarding.

Cool Boarders. From Sony, for Playstation. You'll think you're actually snowboarding—okay, you won't, but you'll wish you were when you play this classic. Currently, there are three different versions of Cool Boarders available.

Courier Crisis. You're a bike messenger on a BMX rig. You have lots of attitude and get into trouble. From GT Interactive, for Playstation. Not a terribly authentic BMX game, but pretty fun.

Nagano Winter. Modeled after the Winter Olympics, this Nintendo 64 game from Konami features one of the best electronic renditions of a snowboard half-pipe. Well worth the money!

Great Extreme Sports Websites 13

O kay, so you think you've learned everything there is to know about extreme sports? Wrong! The world of extreme sports is constantly changing, and the best way to keep up with it is by surfing the internet—where you can find on-line lessons, product reviews, interviews, magazines, terrain and condition reports, and other people who share your extreme attitudes. Here are fifty sites to get you started—you can find a complete listing of sites, updated every day, at Charged, the on-line extreme sports magazine. Just surf over to http://www.charged.com and click on the menu item that says "Cool Sites."

HOW THIS WORKS

We've arranged our sites into five categories: multisport, bike (mountain, BMX, and freestyle), snowboard, skate (board and in-line), and surf. Just type in the URL listed to go to the site. Remember, though, that site addresses do come and go. We've done our best to make sure these are accurate, but some links may not work. That's okay. Just fire up a search engine like Infoseek (http://www.infoseek.com) or Hotbot (http://www.hotbot.com), type in the name of the sport or event you're looking for, and you'll get a fresh list of sites.

Multisport

Adventure sports on-line: This is another site that lists lots of other sites and has direct links to them. A good starting point.

http://www.adventuresports.com

AAAH, the all adrenaline action hitlist: A really functional, well-designed, and very cool listing of the best action sports sites. They offer opinions about the coolest sites—and they're usually right.

http://people.zeelandnet.nl/nas/

Charged: The oldest and maybe the best on-line action sports 'zine, created by the author of this book (so of course we like it!). Check it out for yourself.

http://www.charged.com

Concussion: An on-line version of a print 'zine dedicated to tricks and how to pull them off. Really well designed.

http://www.etheria.com/concussion/home.html

ESPN sportszone: Besides giving some of the best on-line coverage of mainstream sports, there's extensive information here about the X-Games—winter and summer, past and present.

http://www.espn.com

Extreme sports on-line: They own the name "extreme sports," and this site is dedicated to rad dudes, shredders, and

people who like to wear bandannas. Check it out.
http://www.extreme-sports.com

Global snow and surf report (GSSR): Say "geezer" and you'll know how it's pronounced. A massive set of links to weather and conditions info for surfers and boarders. Great if you're planning a weekend trip.
http://www.geezer.com

Great outdoor recreation pages (GORP): This is a more nature and adventure-oriented site. It's huge and well organized. (By the way, Gorp is a 1960s term for trail mix.)
http://www.gorp.com/

MTV: Yep, it's the music video channel—which has a surprisingly good action sports section, as well as tons of stuff about the rest of the network.
http://www.mtv.com

Mountain zone: Another extensive site dedicated to everything—bike, climb, hike, camp, and more—you can do at high altitude. Famous for its live event reports.
http://www.mountainzone.com

BIKES
American Bicycle Association: One of the sanctioning organizations for BMX. Lots of links, resources, tips, and general info for the beginning and advanced BMX/freestyler.
http://www.ababmx.org

Bicycle motocross: A really comprehensive, well-designed BMX resource, with an excellent photo gallery.
http://www.dinamite.com/bmx/

Bikesite: Another super-comprehensive bike resource, with links to everything and anything that has to do with the bicycle world.
http://www.bikesite.com

BMX on-line: Just in case you thought BMX was for the United States only, here's a British site that gives a continental spin on the sport.
http://www.cityscape.co.uk/users/dv59

Bobby's BMX-freestyle world: Maybe the best hand-made site on the internet. Check it out, take it in, and you'll know how to create your own.
http://www-personal.umich.edu/~bkcarter/Bobby's_World2.html

Chunk 666: A site devoted entirely to custom bikes—especially choppers, choppers, and more choppers.
http://www.reed.edu/~karl/chunk/chunk.html

Gearhead: One of the first—and still one of the best—on-line off-road magazines. Lots of product reviews and trail resources.
http://www.gearhead.com

GT bicycles: One of the biggest BMX and mountain bike man-ufacturers has one of the most comprehensive and sophisticated websites.
http://www.gtbicycles.com

Mountain bike daily: The on-line version of *Mountain Bike* magazine. A product review every day, race reports right from the events, back issues, and more.
http://www.mountainbike.com

National bicycle league: The other BMX sanctioning organization, and also a terrific site.
http://www.nbl.org

Skate Sites

Acme skateboards: One of the granddaddy skateboard companies, full of mainline info about riding, equipment, and the pros.
http://www.sk8acme.com

Aloha skateboards: Hawaiian koa hardwood skateboards, long and custom. The prettiest on the planet.
http://www.hawaiian.net/~spanky/

Cops eat donuts: Funny name, great site. Full of places to skate all over the world, complete with events, videos, and music.
http://www.skateboard.co.uk/

Enternet skateboarding videos: Tons of huge skateboard movies. You'll be downloading all night. It's worth it.
http://enternet.com/skate/video.html

Focus: Part of a skateboard web ring—go to this site and you'll automatically be shuttled through cyberspace to other related sites.
http://www.netonecom.net/~nepote/

Grass sole: Dedicated to mountain and all-terrain skateboarding—huge wheels, rocky trails, and more fun than you've ever had.
http://www.iaccess.com.au/grassole/index.html

In-line skating: A very comprehensive, home made site devoted to the sport of in-line. Lots of links, too.
http://www.inlineskate.com

Rollerblade home page: The official homepage for the official in-line company, with really good resources and ideas.
http://www.rollerblade.com

Skateluge and streetluge: These two wild variants on skateboarding are both "official" extreme sports, having recently been added to the X-games.
http://www.skateluge.com

Skategeezer: Want to know about old-school skating? Looking for a sense of history and truth? The skategeezer knows all.
http://www.interlog.com/ ~ mbrooke/skategeezer.html

Snowboard Sites

@Play: Killer snow info site. Nice design, good links. Lots of places to go.
http://www.atplay.com

Burton snowboards: The monster snowboard company. Tons of information. Products, clothes, athletes. Everything. Go. Now.
http://www.burton.com

The dump: A U.K. snowboard magazine. Good listings. Updated very often. Check this out even if you aren't in the UK!
http://www.internexus.co.uk/nwaiag/dump

Flakezine: The best, funniest all-snowboard magazine on the web. No kidding.
http://www.flakezine.com

Fresh and tasty: An on-line snowboard magazine produced by and for women. Really great info, and interesting even if you're not a girl.
http://www.freshandtasty.com

Hyperski: A great site. Extensive information on travel and snow conditions around the world, from Zurmont to Sugarbush. Slick graphics and good articles.
http://www.sssss.com

International snowboarding federation: This is the sport's official sanctioning body. Since some snowboarders feel very unofficial, they don't like this site. Others do. It's worth a visit.
http://www.isf.ch

Snowboarding glossary: Jason Dow is the man with a glossary plan. Nicely done!
http://www2.hawaii.edu/~dow/

Snowboarding on-line: Another huge and great snow-boarding site, with great interactive lessons and tips. Say "SOL" (Soul) and you know what we're talking about.
http://www.solsnowboarding.com

TWS now on-line: Transworld Snowboard and Snowboard Life are both published by the same company. And they share a very thorough website with lots of live event reports.

http://www.twsnow.com

Surf Sites

All about boards: Informative with slick graphics. They even tell you how to custom design and order your own personal board. Don't miss it!

http://www.ifas.ufl.edu/~jrr/irs/boards.html

Learning to surf: The power of text: Chris Payne's how-to-surf FAQ gives you the basics.

http://facs.scripps.edu/surf/12surfII.html

New school surfing: This is the mother of all surf info sites—not to mention great pictures.

http://www.geocities.com/Colosseum/Track/5378/

Surf check: Classic. Graphics quality is low—info quality is amazing. The best wave reports on-line.

http://www.surfcheck.com

Surfer magazine: Only the bible of the sport. The print version of this mag is essential reading for any surfer. The on-line version fills in the blanks, with more resources and info.

http://www.surfermag.com

Surfer girl magazine: Surfer girl cafe, news and environmental reports, and true unbelievable tales from "hardcore, soulful waterwomen."

http://www.surfergirl.com

Surfing museum: An under-construction site that gives you an online version of the surf history location in Santa Cruz, California.

http://www.cruzio.com/arts/scva/surf.html

Surflink: Based in California, with event coverage and—best of all—live cams that monitor the waves at most of the popular beaches in and around Los Angeles.

http://www.surflink.com

Surfrider foundation: Possibly the most important and influential environmental group in the history of extreme sports. Visit, learn, join.

http://www.surfrider.org

Surf video network: Not just surf videos, either—a great source for viewing and purchasing all kinds of extreme sports tapes.

http://www.surfvideo.com

Tsunami: Ever wonder what surfers in Japan are doing? Maybe one day you'll go there—in the meantime, check out this site.

http://www.twics.com/~acjohnst/home.html

From A to X: An Extreme Glossary

Here is a list of common terms you'll find in the extreme sports world. Remember, since extreme sports are very trendy, some of these slang words might be as old as yesterday's news even before you read them! The best way to learn the newest terms is to do the sports yourself. It's an instant vocabulary builder.

How to Use the Glossary

Some terms apply to more than one sport. We've put an abbreviation next to each term to help you figure out which sport it applies to:

(mb) Mountain biking

(sk) Skateboarding

(sn) Snowboarding

(in) In-line skating

(mx) BMX

(su) Surfing

(x) All extreme sports

ABEC (sk, in): A high-quality type of bearing used in skate wheels.

Aggro (x): Short for aggressive. Anybody with a particularly wild, or even reckless, way of practicing an extreme sport would be considered aggro.

Betty/Barney (su): A Betty is a girl. A Barney is a boy. It comes from *The Flintstones* (Betty and Barney Rubble).

the 'Bird (sn): Short for Snowbird; considered by many to be the best place on earth to ride a snowboard; located in Utah.

Board AID (sn): An annual charity event held by snowboarders to raise money for AIDS research. There are similar events in most other extreme sports, and they're a great way to turn your hobby into something good for the world.

bonk (sn, mb): In snowboarding, to "bonk" is to bounce off something, like a picnic table. In mountain biking, you "bonk" when you run out of energy, like after a long ride, on a day you forgot to eat breakfast.

carve (sn): Cutting high-speed turns through the snow on one edge of your snowboard. Riders who are leaning so far in that they're nearly parallel to the snow are "power carving."

deck (sk): The top of your skateboard. Decks come in many sizes and designs. You can paint your own deck if you want. One thing *not* to do is choose your skateboard solely based on the deck graphics. Find one that fits your riding style.

dual suspension (mb): A bike that has shock absorbers in the front and the back. Often used for downhilling, because they're heavier than hardtails (bikes with only front shocks), but a good dual-suspension bike can help you get uphill, too, because it helps "stick" your wheels to the ground.

durometer (sk, in, mb): A measure of softness in rubber. In skating, durometer measurements are used for wheels. In mountain biking, they describe the softness of rubber used in some suspension systems.

The Endless Summer (su): The first true extreme sports movie, *The Endless Summer* (made in the 1960s) was the story of two surfers searching the earth for the perfect wave.

freeride (sn, mb): Riding the way you want, as fancy or as simple as you want, usually with grace and speed. Mountain bikers have begun to use this term, which was once only for snowboarding.

freestyle (mx, x): An offshoot of BMX. It isn't racing—it's just doing the coolest tricks. As with skate tricks, there are both street tricks and ones you do on a ramp or in a park. Also a generic term for doing tricks.

Green Room (su): When there's nothing but ocean water all around you, and the roar of the sea fills your ears, this is where you are.

grip tape (sk): A rough kind of sticky tape that's used on skateboards to help keep your feet on the board. You can also find grip tape on most staircases in your school. (But you can't skateboard on your school's staircase!)

grommet (su, sn): Originally a surfing term, it's spread to snow-boarding. A grommet is a young, enthusiastic beginner. "Grom" is short for grommet.

hockey stop (in): Coming to a sliding halt on your in-line skates. Not easy to do when there's no ice to dig into.

knuckle-dragger (sn): A derogatory term skiers used for snowboard-ers, because of the way they had to push themselves along on flat stretches of snow. An alternate explanation: when power carving at such a steep angle that the boarder's hand actually could touch the snow. Either way, the skiers stopped using the term when they realized snowboarding was so much fun.

liftie (sn): The person who helps people get on and off the lift at a ski area. Getting a job as a liftie is one of the most popular ways com-mitted snowboarders get into the ski business, and they usually get to snowboard for free (employees get passes).

Mavericks (su): One of the best big-wave beaches in the continental United States. It's near Santa Cruz, California, and wave heights there can reach thirty feet.

mountain board (sk): A crazy-looking skateboard meant for blasting down ski slopes. It's got superwide, fat wheels and a big deck.

Rock Shox® (mb): A brand of mountain-bike front suspension that's the world's most popular. Front suspension isn't just a tool—it's a safety item that helps your wheels roll over bumps more smoothly.

Rollerblade® *(in)*: Not a generic term for in-line skates, but many people use the term that way, anyway. It's actually a brand name for the most popular line of in-line skates.

roost (mb, mx): When you're going so fast that tiny puffs of dust appear behind you. Some people say they look like rooster tails.

shaka (su): A Hawaiian term for "cool." If you're hanging out with your buddies and something good happens, you say: "Shaka, brah!" ("Cool, brother!")

shred (x): To go fast, with style.

street (sk, in): A verb for riding in your neighborhood—and making it into an obstacle course.

Stumpjumper (mb): The first truly successful commercial mountain bike. Originally built in the mid-1980s, you can still buy a Stumpjumper today. There's one in the Smithsonian Institution in Washington, D.C.!

titanium (mb): A metal originally used to build airplanes that also is used to make super high-quality, supertough, and superexpensive mountain bikes. You can recognize titanium because it is never painted; instead, it is a polished, gray color.

vert (sk, in): Airborne skate maneuvers, usually in a pool or skate park, or on a neighborhood ramp.

wahine (su): Pronounced "wah-HEE-nee." Hawaiian for a sea goddess, and surf speak for a girl who really knows how to surf. One of the best surfing magazines for women has the same name.

wheelie (mb, mx): When you lift the front end of your bike up and ride on the back wheel only. Essential for getting over obstacles but more fun if you can hold one for a long time. A nose wheelie is the opposite: The back end of the bike goes up and the front stays down (much harder and not sustainable, since you can't pedal forward).

X Games (x): ESPN's twice-a-year televised action extravaganza. The first X Games were not considered very cool by most people in the extreme sports world. But since then ESPN has improved the quality, and now the event is much anticipated by all. There's a summer version and a winter version.

Index

Dan Koeppel is a mountain biker and snowboarder. He writes a monthly column called "Hug the Bunny" for *Mountain Bike* magazine, and is the founder of *Charged*, an interactive on-line action sports magazine. Check it out at http://www.charged.com. Dan has also written for *Transworld Snowboarding, The Los Angeles Times, The New York Times, Audubon, Sports Afield,* and *Travel-Holiday* magazine. He lives in Santa Monica, California.